A Hazard Model of CAMELS Downgrades of Low-Risk Community Banks

Gary Whalen

OCC Economics Working Paper 2005-1

May 2005

A Hazard Model of CAMELS Downgrades of Low-Risk Community Banks[*]

Gary Whalen

Abstract

Over the past 30 years, a great deal of research has investigated the potential usefulness of early warning models as offsite supervisory tools. Accurate offsite models allow bank supervisors to identify high-risk banks at a reasonable length of time prior to marked deterioration in their financial condition, without the use of expensive, time-consuming on-site examinations. This allows scarce examination resources to be used more efficiently and permits supervisory constraints to be imposed or rehabilitative strategies put in place expeditiously and so minimize the risk of costly failures.

This paper develops a Cox proportional hazard model that is designed to predict the probability that a low-risk community bank will be downgraded to high-risk status over an eight-quarter time horizon. The risk dichotomy is made on the basis of CAMELS composite supervisory ratings with a score of 2 separating the low- and high-risk groups. Models are estimated using independent variables measured at year-end 1997, 1998, and 1999. The out-of-sample forecasting accuracy of the estimated models is examined using data for year-end 2001. In general, the hazard models are found to produce relatively accurate risk classifications out-of-sample. The accuracy of the 1997 specification suggests that these hazard models are relatively stable over time, implying that frequent, costly re-specification is not required. The hazard models are also found to be considerably more accurate than two simpler supervisory screens. Taken together the out-of-sample tests of classification accuracy suggest that this sort of statistical model is a promising, relatively low cost early warning tool.

---

[*] The opinions expressed here are those of the author and do not necessarily represent those of the OCC or the Treasury. The author would like to thank Mike Carhill, David Nebhut, and Jeffrey Brown for their comments and Amy Millen for editorial assistance.

Please direct any comments to Gary Whalen, Senior Economic Advisor, Office of the Comptroller of the Currency, 250 E St, SW, Washington, DC 20219, gary.whalen@occ.treas.gov, or (202) 874-4441.

I. Introduction

Over the past 30 years, a great deal of research has investigated the potential usefulness of early warning models as offsite supervisory tools. Accurate offsite models give bank supervisors the capability to identify high-risk banks at a reasonable length of time prior to marked deterioration in their financial condition, without the use of expensive, time-consuming on-site examinations. This allows scarce examination resources to be used more efficiently and permits supervisory constraints to be imposed or rehabilitative strategies put in place expeditiously and so minimize the risk of costly failures.

Statistical models designed to explain or predict measures of bank risk have been the focal point of a considerable number of previous empirical studies. But relatively few of those studies have used a hazard model approach, despite its potential advantages. Only a handful of studies have compared the accuracy of econometric models to simpler supervisory screens. In this paper, several versions of a Cox proportional hazard model are estimated that are designed to predict the likelihood of a CAMELS composite rating downgrade for low- risk community national banks over an eight-quarter time horizon.[1] Annual year-end data are used to estimate the models, beginning in 1997. The accuracy of this model is examined out-of-sample. The out-of-sample analysis includes a comparison between the accuracy of this model and two supervisory screens.

Briefly, the estimated models are relatively accurate in predicting downgrades. Also the Cox models appear to predict downgrades much more accurately than the simpler supervisory screens.

---

[1] The CAMELS composite score is a numerical rating assigned by supervisors to reflect their assessment of the overall financial condition of a bank. The score takes on integer values ranging from 1 (best) to 5 (worst). For a more detailed discussion of the CAMELS score, see Feldman and Schmidt (1999).

The organization of the paper is as follows. In the next section, relevant previous studies are briefly reviewed. In section III, the construction of the Cox models used in the study are detailed. The estimation results are presented in section IV. Model forecasting accuracy is discussed in section V. Section VI presents a summary of the results and conclusions.

II. Previous Research

A large number of previous studies have investigated early warning models for banks. Given the size of this body of work, only the most relevant studies are reviewed here.

A hazard model approach has been used in a relatively small number of previous studies investigating the determinants of alternative measures of bank risk. These include Lane, Looney, and Wansely (1986); Whalen (1991); Fissel (1994); Wheelock and Wilson (2000); and Gropp, Vesala and Vulpes (2002). The first four studies model the risk of bank failure using samples of U.S. banks over various time periods. All five use proportional hazard models, although Fissel estimates a parametric version called a Weibull model.

Only three of these papers (Lane, Looney and Wansely (1986); Whalen (1991); and Gropp, Vesala, and Vulpes (2002)) really are early warning studies that focus on developing and testing the out-of-sample accuracy of models designed to predict bank risk.[2] In the first two of these studies, the event of interest is bank failure, and the models have a maximum time horizon

---

[2] In Fissel (1994), a bank failure model is estimated, but the paper focuses on using the model to develop fair risk-related deposit insurance premiums. In Wheelock and Wilson (2000), the paper explains failure and acquisition in a competing risks framework.

of two years. In general, the set of independent variables found to be significant consist of ratios constructed from regulatory call reports that are standard indicators of dimensions of bank risk.[3]

Unlike the other two studies, Gropp, et al. attempt to model the risk of a non-supervisory ratings downgrade for a relatively small sample of European Union (EU) banks. More specifically, they define a downgrade as a reduction in a bank's Fitch-IBCA financial strength rating to a grade of C or below. Given the stated definition of a C-level rating, this risk dichotomy is similar to the approach used in this paper.[4] They note the benefits of using such a risk measure in early warning models when failures are rare. The focus in their paper is on whether or not variables constructed from equity and bond market price and yield data are useful leading indicators of the risk of publicly traded banks.

In general, the hazard models produce reasonably accurate forecasts of bank risk out-of-sample. But the issue of forecasting accuracy across model types is not typically explored in great detail in any of these studies.

Only a limited number of studies compare the relative accuracy of statistical early warning models and supervisory screens. One such study is Gilbert, Meyer and Vaughan (1999). The authors survey both supervisors and existing literature to obtain a list of 14 potential risk indicators. They compare the forecasting accuracy of each of these individual screening variables and a statistical model in which these variables are used as explanatory variables. They

---

[3] Whalen (1991) also found that the lagged percentage change in the state level housing permits was a significant predictor of bank failure risk.

[4] A C-rated bank is defined as "an adequate bank that, however, possesses one or more troublesome aspects." See Gropp, Vesala and Vulpes (2002), appendix 2, p.53. Banks with composite ratings of 3 "… exhibit some degree of supervisory concern in one or more … areas." See Federal Reserve Commercial Bank Examination Manual (1997), A.5020.1, p.2.

examine the relative abilities of these screens and model to identify both failures (1989-1991) and CAMELS 1 and 2 rated banks that are downgraded (1991-1997).[5]

First they examine the ability of individual screen variables to identify low-risk banks that fail 12 to 24 months in the future. They rank banks with CAMELS ratings of 2 at a given year-end by the value of each screen variable from highest risk to lowest risk and calculate the percentage of banks that would have to be examined using the screen variable as a guide to flag one-half of the failures. They find that a number of individual screens are superior to a random examination strategy. Then they use estimates of failure probabilities over the period 12 to 24 months in the future from a logit model to rank CAMELS 2 rated banks from highest to lowest risk. They find that the failure model also is superior to a random examination strategy in identifying subsequent failures.

Next, they compare the accuracy of the individual screens to that of the failure model for three different out-of-sample forecast periods. They find that the accuracy rankings of the screen variables change over time. In each forecast year, the best screen variable is about as accurate as the model, but the best screen variable changes year-to-year and so would not be known *a priori*. They conclude on average over the three-year period that the model is significantly more accurate than the individual screens in identifying low-risk banks that subsequently failed. They also examine the relative abilities of the four best screens and the model to identify accurately CAMELS 2 rated banks that did not fail out-of-sample. This analysis reveals that no one screen consistently outperforms the model.

They also investigate whether screens or a statistical model are better able to correctly identify low-risk banks that suffered downgrades in their supervisory ratings during the 1991 to

---

[5] In the rating system used by bank supervisors, bank condition and risk are reflected in the assigned composite rating and the individual component ratings. The ratings are integer values ranging from 1, indicating best condition or least risk to 5, indicating worst condition or highest risk.

1997 period. Specifically they focus on predicting downgrades of CAMELS 1 or 2 rated banks to a CAMELS rating of 3, 4, or 5 12 to 24 months in the future.[6] They compare the out-of-sample classification accuracy of the individual screens and a logit model that includes the entire set of 14 variables. Again, they rank banks in each forecast period from highest estimated risk to lowest based on either a given screen or downgrade probability generated by the statistical model. Alternatively assuming that supervisors examine banks based on these rankings, they compare the percentage of banks that must be examined to identify half of the downgrades in each forecast period. They find that the model is considerably more accurate than all of the screens. For example, they report that on average over the seven forecast years analyzed, exams based on model-generated risk rankings would identify half of the CAMELS 2 banks downgraded if only 18 percent of banks of sample were examined. As was the case when accuracy in identifying future failures was investigated, the best single screen in flagging downgrades varies over time. But the single best screen would require that an average of roughly 31 percent of banks be examined to identify correctly half of the downgrades.

The study by Cole, Cornyn and Gunther (1995) also compares the forecasting accuracy of statistical early warning models and screens. In this study, the statistical model is designed to predict a bank's composite CAMELS rating at a one-quarter time horizon.[7] Technically the model is an ordered logit model and generates estimates of the probability that each bank has each of the five possible CAMELS composite values. Model predictions are based on the expected CAMELS score, which is obtained by multiplying each possible CAMELS score by the estimated probability and then summing the products. The set of independent variables used in

---

[6] Since they do not use a hazard model approach, they are forced to exclude all low-risk banks that suffer downgrades over the 0-12 month time horizon from their samples.

[7] The study also includes an analysis of a statistical model that is designed to predict failures over a two-year time horizon. The failure model is less germane here and so is not discussed.

this model includes standard risk indicator ratios constructed from call reports, lagged CAMELS composite and management component ratings, and two elements of the Uniform Bank Surveillance System (UBSS) supervisory screen used by the Federal Reserve System until 1993. The predictions of this model are compared with those based solely on the UBSS screen composite score. This composite score is constructed from four component ratios for each of nine asset size-based peer groups.[8] For each peer group, banks are ranked on the basis of each of the four ratios from best to worst and receive the corresponding percentile score. Then the equally weighted sum of these four percentile scores is calculated for each bank. The peer group banks are ranked on the basis of this sum, and the corresponding percentile value is their UBSS composite score.

The authors report different comparisons of forecast accuracy of the screen and the statistical model in their study. The most relevant one is where both tools are used to forecast the downgrades of CAMELS 1 and 2 rated banks to ratings of 3, 4, or 5 in a number of different out-of-sample forecast periods.[9] They conclude that the statistical model outperforms the supervisory screen in predicting downgrades.[10]

III. The Construction of the Model

IIIa. The Measure of Risk

---

[8] Two other secondary screens, also percentile rankings, are used in the UBSS. The first is based on asset growth over the previous four quarters, the other on the cost of volatile liabilities. The asset growth score is the other UBSS component that is used as an explanatory variable in the statistical CAMELS prediction model.

[9] Specifically, they look at quarterly forecasts from 1989:Q4 – 1992:Q1.

[10] See Cole, Cornyn and Gunther (1995), pp. 12-13.

Statistical early warning models can be designed to produce estimates of different indices of bank risk. Each of these potential risk measures has associated advantages and disadvantages. In this study, the target bank risk measure is based on supervisory ratings. More precisely, the model developed is designed to produce estimates of the probability that a "low-risk" bank is subsequently downgraded to "high-risk" status over an eight-quarter time period. Banks are designated "low-risk" if they have a CAMELS composite score of 1 or 2. Banks with composite CAMELS scores above 2 are classified as high-risk.

Advantages and disadvantages are associated with using supervisory ratings-based measures of risk in a statistical early warning model. The main advantage of this sort of approach is that exam ratings are thought to be highly accurate measures of bank condition (at least of current condition), since they reflect supervisory assessments of private information (e.g., on the quality of non-traded loans and the institution's management) that may be superior to that available to outside analysts. In addition, accurate CAMELS prediction or downgrade models are useful to supervisors. Identifying low-risk banks likely to be downgraded implies that supervisors have time to limit any moral hazard behavior or assist in the rehabilitation of the institution. Downgrade models might also be used to select the apparently low-risk banks that should be examined sooner rather than later.

A number of disadvantages also are associated with using supervisory assessments when modeling bank risk. One is that such ratings reflect subjective judgments by examiners, and these judgments may differ across banks or change over time (e.g., banks in different size classes might be rated according to different criteria, or examination standards could change for all banks over time). Also the precise linkage between the ratings and expected condition at some point in the future can be unclear. For example, a composite score of 5 indicates a high likelihood of failure within a relatively short time, despite preventative measures. The signals provided by CAMELS scores of 3 and 4 are less clear, as is the incremental impact of moving up or down the rating scale by 1 or more rating points. Further, when model predictions and actual ratings disagree, it is not clear which is the correct indicator of a bank's true risk.

Yet another potential problem, especially in the case of early warning hazard models that explicitly focus on the timing of the risk event, is that ratings reflect supervisory judgments about a bank's condition at a particular moment in time. Historically, such assessments have been made only on the basis of an onsite full scope exam. Since such exams typically recur with a lag of four quarters or more, and the length of the lag might reflect any number of factors, the point in time at which supervisors recognize a change in bank risk in the form of a rating revision might not necessarily coincide closely with the point in time at which the change in risk could have been discerned if the bank was examined earlier. This problem, however, has been mitigated in recent years by the adoption of quarterly "periodic monitoring" of national banks by supervisors.[11] This monitoring can be offsite and can result in changes in supervisory ratings and onsite exam timing. As a result, exam ratings are likely to be better contemporaneous risk indicators than they have been in the past.

Another potential problem with ratings-based risk measures is that it may be difficult to estimate reliable models during periods when there are few banks in some ratings classes or when few downgrades occur. This circumstance, however, is not unique to this sort of risk measure, and in fact, appears to be a much less serious problem especially in recent periods than if a failure-based risk measure was used instead.

---

[11] For a description of the periodic monitoring process for national banks, see "Community Bank Supervision," *Comptroller's Handbook* (July 2003), pp. 137-140.

To summarize, a CAMELS downgrade model is estimated in this paper.[12] More specifically, a model is estimated that generates estimates of the probability that a bank rated 1 or 2 at a given year-end is subsequently downgraded to a 3, 4, or 5 over the eight-quarter period beginning in the second quarter of the subsequent year.[13] Over the time periods examined, the numbers of observed downgrades appear to be sufficient to produce reliable model estimates.

III.b. The Hazard Downgrade Model

The focus of any hazard model is the time that elapses from the moment that observation of the sample subjects begins until the occurrence of some event of interest, the subject exits the sample, or the period of observation ends. Conventionally, subjects that experience the event during the interval of observation are referred to as "failures," and so the time measurement is also referred to as "time to failure." Conversely, those that do not experience the event are referred to as "survivors." Subjects that disappear from the sample before the end of the period of observation without experiencing the event or that survive through the end of the period are referred to as "censored." One advantage of the hazard model approach relative to logit models is that it permits censored observations to be included in the estimation sample.

The time to failure for the collection of subjects in the sample is assumed to be a random variable with a probability distribution. The probability distribution of time to failure can be expressed in different ways. One convenient way to express this probability distribution is the

---

[12]Other possible risk indicators (e.g., private market debt ratings or measures based on equity or bond prices) could be the focus of early warning models, but generally are relevant only for larger banking companies and were not considered.

[13] The one quarter lag is used to reflect the fact that year-end financial data is not available until the first quarter of the subsequent year. So downgrades during the first quarter after the year-end used to estimate the models are excluded from the analysis.

through the related hazard function. A hazard function for a particular value of event time gives the instantaneous risk that an event will occur at the given time, t, for a subject with a given set of characteristics, given that the subject has not experienced the event prior to t.

There are a number of different hazard models that might be used in the analysis, which vary somewhat in form and make different assumptions about how the hazard varies over time. In this paper, various estimated versions of a Cox proportional hazards model are used. In the case of a Cox model, the hazard function has the following general form:

(1) $h(t|X_j) = h_0(t)\exp(X_j B)$

$h(t|X_j) =$ the instantaneous risk of an event for subject j at time t, given its relevant characteristics reflected in the set of variables included in X.

$h_0(t) =$ the baseline hazard for time period t

$X_j B =$ X_j represents a vector of variables describing relevant characteristics of subject j presumed to influence the hazard, and B represents a corresponding vector of weights that describe how each characteristic variable influences the hazard.

Another way to express this same probability distribution of event times is through the related survivor function. The survivor function gives the probability that a subject with a given set of relevant characteristics will not experience the event of interest through time t, or will survive beyond t. In the case of a Cox model, the survivor function has the form given by equation 2:

(2) $S(t|X_j) = S_0(t)^{q_j}$

$S(t|X_j) =$ the probability that subject j with characteristics given by X_j does not experience the event or survives through t, the chosen time horizon.

$S_0(t) =$ the "baseline" survival probability for the chosen time horizon t.

$q_j =$ an equation that incorporates the estimated coefficients or weights that describe how each included characteristic variable in X_j affects the probability that subject j survives beyond t.

The formula for q_j, in turn, is given in equation 3:

(3) $q_j = \exp(X_j B)$

where $X_j B$ has the same definition as it does in equation (1) above.

In the Cox model, the baseline hazard and survival probabilities are the same for all subjects and depend only on time. This specification implies that the ratio of the hazards of any two subjects is constant over time and is the reason this specification is called a proportional hazard model.[14] The results of model estimation are the estimates of the baseline probabilities and the coefficients or weights on the characteristic variables that indicate the effect of each included variable on the likelihood that a subject experiences the event of interest. The estimation also provides measures of the statistical significance of each included characteristic variable and the entire set of variables taken together. This provides insight on the degree of confidence that can be placed on the coefficient estimates and the generated failure or survival probabilities that they imply.

Several reasons explain why hazard models are preferable to alternatives like the binary logit model. Unlike the logit model, hazard models take the timing of events over the interval of observation into account. Hazard models also permit the inclusion of subjects that are censored in the estimation sample. The Cox proportional hazard model also offers a potential advantage over alternative hazard models in that no assumption is made about how the baseline hazard

---

[14] For a more complete discussion of hazard models, see Cleves, Gould and Gutierrez (2002); Allison (1995); or Hosmer and Lemeshow (1999). There are statistical tests to determine if the proportional hazard assumption is valid. The results of one such test is discussed later.

varies over time.[15] This is appropriate when there is no strong *a priori* reason to expect a particular relationship, which appears to be the case here.[16]

To go from the general to the specific, in this paper the event of interest is the downgrade of a bank initially classified as low-risk to high-risk status during the period of observation. Event time is measured in quarters and the interval of observation is eight quarters beginning one quarter after the year-end marking the date at which the characteristic variables are measured. So for each bank the time to downgrade can range from one quarter to a maximum of eight quarters. Each estimated survivor function yields the probability that a low-risk national bank with a given set of characteristics at a given year-end will not be downgraded to high-risk status through the end of each of eight subsequent quarters beginning one quarter after the start of the observation period.

Conveniently, the survival probabilities produced by these models can be viewed as an indicator of financial strength. For example, survival probabilities close to 1 (the upper bound) imply low probabilities of the low-risk bank being downgraded over a particular eight-quarter period.

III.c. The Data Sets Used to Estimate the Model

For simplicity and to permit a reasonable test of out-of-sample forecast accuracy, models are estimated using only year-end annual data for 1997, 1998, and 1999 for the explanatory

---

[15] For example, the exponential model and Weibull model are also proportional hazard models, but embody particular assumptions about the relationship between the hazard rate and time. In the former the hazard is constant over time. In the latter the relationship between the hazard and time can vary.

[16] Other types of hazard models, called parametric hazard models, exist where a specific relationship between the hazard and time are assumed. These sorts of models can produce more precise estimates of the effects of the included variables if the data are consistent with the assumed relationship.

variables. The estimation sample for each time period consists of low-risk national banks with total assets of $1 billion or less. Credit card banks, banks in existence less than three years, banks that were never examined over the eight-quarter time horizon, and banks that were downgraded or disappeared during the first quarter of the subsequent year were excluded from all samples.

For each of the three year-ends, sample banks were followed over the eight-quarter period beginning with the second quarter of the subsequent year. Each bank in the sample was assigned a time value representing the number of quarters that elapsed between the start of the interval and either the quarter in which it was downgraded or disappeared for some other reason. Banks that were not downgraded over the entire period were assigned a maximum time value of eight quarters.[17]

A similar data set was also constructed using year-end data for 2001. This data set is used to test the out-of-sample forecasting accuracy of the models estimated for the three earlier time periods.

III.d. The Explanatory Variables Used

The usefulness of a large number of potential explanatory variables was investigated in this study. Most of the set of variables examined are standard indicators of bank risk and return constructed from call reports. Only year-end values of these ratios were used. But the potential usefulness of variables drawn from several additional sources was also investigated. These include supervisory information (the existence of informal and formal enforcement actions, assessments of management quality, time from last full scope exam), market structure data

---

[17] Technically, the latter two groups of banks are treated as censored in the analysis.

13

(drawn from FDIC Summary of Deposit files), and state-level economic data drawn from several sources.

The results of previous research, judgment, and preliminary statistical analysis were used to cull a relatively small set of the most informative variables from the original large set of data. The variables that appear in the final form of the estimated equations chosen for each time period are statistically significant, exhibit reasonable coefficient signs, together comprise a statistically significant model, and ultimately were found to do a reasonably good job of forecasting downgrade probabilities out-of-sample. Virtually all of the variables found to be significant in this study are ratios that have been shown to be informative risk predictors in previous work. A more detailed discussion of the signs and significance of the coefficients on the included variables appear in the following section.

IV. Estimation of the Hazard Models

The first column of table 1 contains the results for the "best" Cox model estimated using year-end 1997 data for the explanatory variables and downgrade information for the 1998:Q2 – 2000:Q1 interval. This model is labeled the "1997 Model" in table 1. The second column of table 1 contains the "best" model found using 1998 data for the independent variables and downgrade information for the 1999:Q2 – 2001:Q1 interval ("1998 Model"). The third column of table 1 is the "1999 Model" – the best model found using year-end 1999 data and downgrade information for 2000:Q2 – 2002:Q1.

In general, the results in table 1 show that the chosen independent variables in each model are significant individually and collectively. Comparing the results for 1997, 1998, and

1999 also suggests that the downgrade model is relatively stable. Most of the variables in the 1997 model retain their significance when the downgrade model is re-estimated using data from subsequent years. But there are some instances when explanatory variables are found to be significant in one period but not in the other, even though the base periods are separated by only four quarters. Some of this apparent instability may simply reflect the effects of multicollinearity. A truer test of the effects of model instability is the relative forecasting accuracy of the alternative model specifications out-of-sample that is examined later.

The proportional hazard assumption was also explicitly tested as well. The test results support the use of the proportional hazard model.[18]

The list of explanatory variables that appear in the estimated models is a relatively short one. Most are ratios constructed from regulatory call reports filed by all banks. Most of these ratios, or some related variant, consistently appear in many of the models estimated in previous empirical studies because they reflect some aspect of bank risk.

The first variable appearing in all of the models is the ratio of total equity to total assets (EQAR). The risk of a downgrade should be lower for banks with higher capital ratios. This expectation is confirmed by the negative coefficient on EQAR in all of the estimated equations.[19]

The next six explanatory variables in the table are indicators of credit risk. The first of these ratios is total nonperforming loans relative to total loans (TNPLR).[20] The second and third ratios break TNPLR into two component parts. One component is total noncurrent loans divided by total loans (TNCLR); the other is loans past due 30-89 days divided by total loans

---

[18] The test used is the one implemented in the stphtest command in STATA. The separate tests for each independent variable, as well as the global test indicate that the proportional hazard assumption is valid for the estimated model. For a further discussion of this test, see Cleves, Gould, and Gutierrez (2002), pp. 160-162.

[19] Note that coefficient signs appear to be counter-intuitive, since the analysis is being conducted in terms of the survivor function. But this is not the case because the signs on estimated coefficients actually reflect the effect of each independent variable on the risk of the downgrade event or hazard.

[20] The numerator of this variable includes nonaccrual loans, and all loans more than 30 days past due, but still accruing.

(TPD3089LR).[21] The estimation results supported the use of the disaggregated components only in 1999.[22]

The next of the credit risk variables is loan loss provision divided by total assets (PLLR). The fifth credit risk variable is total commercial loans divided by total assets (COMLR), and the last is the reserve for loan losses divided by total loans (RLLR). Higher values of the first five variables imply greater credit risk, while the opposite is true for RLLR. Since banks with more credit risk are more likely to be downgraded, the estimated coefficients on the first five variables should be positive while the coefficient on RLLR should be negative. The estimation results in all three equations are in line with these *a priori* expectations.

The next five ratios in the table can be interpreted as measures of liquidity, although several might also be viewed as indicators of a bank's cost of funds. The first of these variables is total non-maturity deposits divided by total assets (NMDR).[23] The numerator of this ratio is the sum of transactions deposits, savings deposits, and money market deposit accounts. The higher a bank's NMDR, the greater its liquidity and the lower the risk of a downgrade. The estimated negative coefficient on this variable is consistent with this expectation. The next two ratios capture reliance on more volatile liabilities. They are defined as brokered deposits divided by total assets (BROKDR), and borrowed funds with less than 1 year to maturity divided by total assets (OBFLT1YR), respectively. Higher ratios of volatile liabilities imply less liquidity and a higher downgrade risk. The estimated coefficients on OBFLT1YR and BROKDR exhibit the expected positive sign, although the latter is significant only in the 1997 model. The next two ratios, total investment securities divided by total assets (TSECR) and pledged securities divided by total securities (PLEDGR) are indicators of the liquidity of the asset side of the balance sheet.

---

[21] Noncurrent loans are the sum of nonaccrual loans and loans past due 90 days or more.
[22] The two coefficients are significantly different from one another in 1999 at the 10 percent level.
[23] This variable is similar to a core deposit ratio, but excludes small time deposits.

Higher values of TSECR and lower values of PLEDGR imply greater liquidity and a lower

downgrade risk, so the expected signs of the coefficients of the two variables are negative and

positive, respectively.   Both exhibit the expected signs, but are significant in only a single year.

Pre-tax return on assets (PTROA), a measure of profitability, is also one of the

explanatory variables appearing in the models.[24] More profitable banks are less like to be

downgraded, and this effect is reflected in the negative coefficient on PTROA in all three of the

estimated equations.

The estimation results reveal that a bank size measure, the log of total assets (LASSET),

also has a significant influence on the probability that a bank is downgraded in all three periods.

The negative significant coefficient probably reflects an actual or perceived size-related

diversification benefit.

The ratio of net gains on loans sold divided by total assets (NGLSR) also was found to be

a significant positive influence on the likelihood that a bank was downgraded in the first two

equations. This variable has not been found to be an important determinant of bank risk in

previous work. The explanation for this result is not clear. It may mean that supervisors view

loan sales as the resort of banks with weakening performance. It could also reflect a belief that

the quality of the portfolio of retained loans is being reduced by the sale of higher quality assets.

The second-to-last explanatory variable listed in table 1 is a measure of interest rate risk.

This variable is defined as total assets repricing in 15 years or more divided by total assets

(TAGT15YR) and is significant only in the 1998 model. Higher values of this ratio imply

greater risk, and so the positive coefficient on this variable conforms with *a priori* expectations.

---

[24] Pretax ROA is used to avoid biases in the use of after tax profitability measures given the growing number of Subchapter S community banks over this interval. For a description of the financial effects of Subchapter S status, see Harvey and Padget (2000).

The final variable that appears in all three models is an indicator of management quality, derived from proprietary exam data (MGTCAM). This variable is a dummy variable and takes on a value of 1 for banks where the management component score exceeds its composite CAMELS rating. Thus banks with values of 1 for this variable have lower management quality. Banks with lower management quality are more likely to suffer downgrades, and this is confirmed by the positive significant coefficients on MGTCAM.

V. Analysis of Model Accuracy

The most meaningful tests of the classification accuracy of any early warning model are out-of-sample tests.[25] To evaluate classification accuracy, predicted risk classifications must be generated using the estimated models. Technically the estimated survivor functions can produce estimates of the likelihood that a bank with given characteristics will survive any number of quarters up to a maximum of eight without being downgraded. When evaluating forecasting accuracy, the focus in this paper is solely on the last quarter of the interval or alternatively on predictions of the probability that a bank with some set of characteristics survives beyond or is not downgraded over the ensuing eight quarters.

To obtain predicted risk classifications, a critical survival probability cutoff threshold must be selected to separate banks with predicted "high" downgrade risks from those with "low" risk. Banks with predicted survival probabilities less than or equal to the critical cutoff value are classified as high risk or predicted downgrades. Those with predicted survival probabilities above the critical value are classified as low risk or a predicted non-downgrade. Once this is

---

[25] That is using the estimated model to predict downgrades for banks held out of the estimation sample and/or data from sample banks over a different time period.

done, these predictions can be compared with actual outcomes to determine the frequency of correct and incorrect classifications made using the model.

Two types of classification error can be made using any early warning model. One is when the model predictions fail to correctly identify true high-risk banks. In this study this means classifying an actual downgrade as a non-downgrade. Conventionally this is called a Type I error. The other sort of error is when the model misclassifies a true low-risk bank as high risk. Here this means predicting that a true non-downgrade will be downgraded. Both of these sorts of errors are of concern when analyzing the accuracy of early warning models. The costs of Type I errors are obvious. But if offsite early warning models are used to assist in the allocation of supervisory resources, they should not incorrectly flag large numbers of true low-risk banks as warranting closer scrutiny. So desirable early warning models generate both low Type I and Type II error rates.

The analysis of the accuracy of early warning models is complicated because changing the probability cutoff value used to make predicted risk classifications changes the number of predicted high-risk and low-risk banks. Raising the critical survival probability cutoff value implies more predicted downgrades, and vice versa. As a result, the assessed classification accuracy of this or any other early warning model varies with the chosen probability cutoff.

One way to proceed is to examine forecast accuracy using some judgmentally chosen probability cutoff value or range of values.[26] An alternative is to calculate all possible combinations of Type I and Type II error rates produced by the model as the classification cutoff value is allowed to vary over virtually all of its entire range from 0 to 1. The graph of all of

---

[26] For example, often the probability is set equal to the relative frequency of high-risk or low-risk banks observed in the estimation sample.

these pairs of error rates is known as a power curve. This is the basic approach taken here and is described in more detail later.

The out-of-sample data set consists of year-end 2001 data for the explanatory variables that appear in the three models for low-risk national banks with total assets of less than $1 billion and downgrade information over the 2002:Q2 – 2004:Q1 period. This sample consists of 1,637 banks. Of these a total of 81 were downgraded by the end of the period of observation. For each downgrade model examined, the probability that a sample bank would not be downgraded by the end of the eight-quarter time period is computed. Then the sample of banks is ranked from predicted highest risk to predicted lowest risk based on the computed probabilities of each model. Next the probability cutoff value is alternatively assumed to be equal to each predicted survival probability observed. For each successive threshold, all banks with probabilities of not being downgraded equal to or less than that threshold are predicted to be high risk, and those with probabilities above this value are predicted to be low risk. The implied Type I and Type II error rates produced by the model for each cutoff value are computed.

This exercise amounts to creating a series of ever larger "watch lists" where each list includes all banks with probabilities less than or equal to each respective probability threshold value. The risk ranking data also reveal how many true high-risk and low-risk banks will be on a watch list of any given size. More accurate models will correctly identify a given percentage of true high-risk banks with a shorter watch list. Alternatively, more accurate models have a lower Type II error rate for any given Type I error rate.

V.a. The Accuracy of the Hazard Models

20

Risk rankings were created using each of the three models in table 1. Table 2 contains the Type I and Type II error rates associated with a small number of watch lists of differing sizes drawn from the risk ranking generated when the 1997 model is used to predict downgrades.[27] Tables 3 and 4 present the same information produced using the 1998 and 1999 models, respectively. In addition, another ranking was also created using a model with the same set of explanatory variables used in the 1997 model specification, but with the coefficients re-estimated using year-end 1999 data for the explanatory variables. This model is referred to as the "1997 Model/1999 Weights" in the paper. This last model is included to illustrate the accuracy obtainable when the specification of the hazard model is fixed over a relatively lengthy period, but where the weights on the explanatory variables are updated periodically. The Type I and Type II error rates generated using this model for several watch list sizes appear in table 5. Thus, the pairs of error rates in the table for each of the models represent five of the large number of points on its complete power curve.

The first row of table 2 shows the Type I and Type II error rates associated with a watch list of the 300 riskiest community banks based on predicted eight-quarter survival probabilities generated using the 1997 model. The associated Type I error rate reveals that a watch list of this relatively small size, focusing on 18.3 percent of all sample banks (300/1637), would correctly identify 62 percent of banks actually downgraded (50/81) and miss 38 percent (31/81). The Type II error rate of 16 percent implies that the watch list includes 249 banks that were not downgraded by the end of 2004:Q1. The results in the rest of the table show the impact of expanding the size of the watch list generated using this model. Expanding the size of the watch list, or alternatively raising the survival probability threshold used to make the risk classifications, generally increases the number of high-risk banks correctly identified (reduces

---

[27] So each row of these tables represent five points on the power curve for each model.

21

the Type I error rate) at the cost of a growing number of misclassifications of low-risk banks (increase in the Type II error rate). The last row of table 2 shows that with a watch list of 500 banks (30.5 percent of the sample), 71.6 percent of high-risk banks are correctly identified (58/81) and 28.4 percent are misidentified (23/81). This watch list would include 442 banks that were not downgraded by the end of 2004:Q1 implying a Type II error rate of 28.4 percent.

The data in table 3 illustrate the out-of-sample classification accuracy of the 1998 model. Since the 1998 model represents a re-specification of the 1997 model, and has re-estimated weights on the explanatory variables, the expectation is that the former should be more accurate than the latter when predicting risk based on more recent 2001 data. But the results in table 3 indicate that this is not the case. For every watch list size examined, the Type I error rate of the 1998 model exceeds that of the 1997 model by several percentage points, and the Type II error rate is slightly higher as well. Still the 1998 model accurately identifies roughly 70 percent of the downgrades and non-downgrades accurately when the watch list size is 500.

Table 4 presents the same information for the 1999 model. Like the 1998 model, the 1999 model represents both a change in specification and change in the explanatory variable weights relative to the 1997 model. In this case, for watch list sizes of 400 and above, the 1999 model is a bit more accurate than both the 1997 and 1998 models in identifying downgrades out-of-sample, with Type I error rates at least one to two percentage points below the older models. The Type II error rates of all three models are roughly the same for all of the watch list sizes examined.

Table 5 shows the results of retaining the specification of the 1997 model and only updating the variable weights using 1999 data. This sort of model adjustment is simpler and so somewhat less costly than a complete re-specification. Comparing the results in tables 2 and 5 reveals that updating only the model coefficients produced very little change in model accuracy. That is, the accuracy of the 1997 model and the 1997 model with 1999 weights is roughly the same.

Taken together, the classification results suggest that these relatively simple statistical models could be useful early warning tools. Each of the models does a reasonably good job of identifying both low- and high-risk banks out-of-sample.[28] The slight differences in accuracy observed when the more recent models are compared with the 1997 model suggest that hazard early warning models are stable, although it is possible that this result reflects the generally benign operating environment for banks in recent years. Stable models are preferable since stability implies lower development and maintenance costs.

V.b. Comparing the Cox Models and a Simpler Supervisory Screen

Additional valuable insights on the usefulness of these statistical early warning models can be gained by comparing their accuracy to simpler supervisory screens. Statistical models tend to be more accurate than simple screens, but also are more complex and costly to construct and use. Comparing the accuracy of the two types of models reveals the nature of the tradeoff between model accuracy and cost.

V.c. Forecasting Downgrades with the Supervisory Screen

---

[28] In fact, the models are relatively successful in identifying banks downgraded beyond the eiqht-quarter forecast period ending in 2004:Q1. For example, using 2001 data in the 1997 model, 12 or the 22 banks (54.5 percent) downgraded over the 2004:Q2 – 2004:Q4 appear on the watch list of 400 banks. The watch list of 450 banks produced using this model contains 14 of the 22 downgrades (63.6 percent). In table 2, these banks are counted as Type II errors since the model predicts them to be downgraded by the end of 2004:Q1.

The accuracy of each of the estimated Cox models is compared with predictions based on the CANARY supervisory screen used by the OCC. In this system, 15 financial indicators are used to measure the credit, interest rate, and liquidity risk of community banks at the end of each quarter.[29] The individual risk measures were chosen judgmentally.

"Static" risk scores are generated for each indicator by comparing the actual value with a level benchmark value that is also judgmentally chosen to separate high-risk from low-risk banks. Banks with indicator values in the high-risk zone are assigned a risk score of 1 for that measure. Rate-of-change risk scores are also generated by comparing the change in the value of each indicator over a four-quarter time horizon with a judgmentally determined rate-of-change benchmark.[30] Again, if the rate-of-change value for a particular indicator falls in the high-risk zone, a risk score of 1 is assigned.

These individual indicators can be combined to produce summary measures of overall risk for banks. Here only two summary measures are examined. The first summary measure of overall risk is the unweighted sum of all 15 static risk scores for each bank. The other is also the unweighted sum of static risk scores, but only for indicators where the bank also has a rate-of-change risk score of 1. The first measure is labeled "static sum" and the second "static/change sum" in this paper.

These summary risk measures can be used to produce overall risk rankings like those generated using the statistical models. For example, banks can be ranked by the descending value of the static sum measure, and the associated Type I and Type II errors resulting from

---

[29] The indicators are adjusted loan loss reserve divided by adjusted loans, a portfolio mix change variable, the rate of loan growth, loans divided by total assets, loans divided by total equity, the gross yield on loans, asset depreciation divided by Tier 1 capital, long-term assets divided by total assets, nonmaturity deposits divided by long-term assets, residential real estate divided by total assets, loans divided by deposits, a measure of net non-core funding dependence, net liquid assets divided by total liabilities, a measure of wholesale funding dependence, and net short-term liabilities divided by total assets.

[30] The rate-of-change risk measures are calculated only for banks that exceeded the median value of the indicator four quarters ago.

varying the critical cutoff value could be computed as described previously. But in practice, using only the value of these summary measures to risk rank the banks in the forecast sample results in a large number of ties. To produce a more informative ranking, banks with a given CANARY-based summary risk score are then ranked in descending order by the forecast expected value of their composite CAMELS generated by the FDIC's SCOR model.[31] Then this ranking is used to produce the Type I and Type II error rates associated with watch lists of varying size that are compared with those resulting from the estimated hazard models.

Table 6 contains the Type I and Type II error rates for the same watch list sizes used in the earlier tables when the static sum measure (in conjunction with the SCOR value) is used to produce the risk rankings. The same information based on the static/change sum risk ranking is presented in table 7. Comparing the Type I error rates in tables 6 and 7 with those in tables 2 through 5 clearly shows that the estimated hazard models are all considerably more accurate in identifying high risk banks out-of-sample than those based on the Canary indicators. For example, using a watch list size of 300 banks, the worst Cox model has a Type I error rate of 40.7 percent (misses 33 of 81 downgrades), while the best Canary-based summary risk measure results in a Type I error rate of 66.7 percent (misses 54 of 81 downgrades). The accuracy advantage of the hazard models is evident for all of the other watch list sizes as well. That is, for every watch list size, the Type I error rate of all of the hazard models is at least 12 percentage points lower than that resulting from the use of the best Canary-based summary risk measure.

Comparison of the Type II error rates in tables 6 and 7 with those in tables 2 through 5 shows that the hazard models are also more accurate in identifying low-risk banks, although the differences in accuracy are considerably smaller. For example, for a watch list size of 300, the Type II error rates of the hazard models are roughly 16 percent vs. 17.5 percent for the Canary-

---

[31] The SCOR model developed by the FDIC produces estimates of CAMELS ratings.

based summary risk measures. For the larger watch list sizes examined, the Type II error rate advantage of the hazard models persists but is less than 1 percentage point.

To summarize, the analysis clearly shows that the estimated hazard models are more accurate than two simpler supervisory screens in identifying both high- and low-risk banks out-of-sample. For all of the watch list sizes examined, the Type I error rates of the hazard models are at least 12 percentage points below those of the two screens, indicating much greater accuracy in flagging banks that experience ratings downgrades. The Type II error rates of the hazard models are roughly 1 percentage point lower than those resulting from classifications based on the supervisory screens. These results show considerable accuracy gains associated with using the more complicated and costly statistical model.

VI. Summary and Conclusions

This paper develops a Cox proportional hazard model that is designed to predict the probability that a low-risk community bank will be downgraded to high-risk status over an eight-quarter time horizon. The risk dichotomy is made on the basis of CAMELS composite supervisory ratings with a score of 2 separating the low- and high-risk groups. Models are estimated using independent variables measured at year-end 1997, 1998, and 1999 and downgrade data for eight quarters after each of these dates. The out-of-sample forecasting accuracy of these models is examined using similar data for year-end 2001 and compared with risk classifications based on two simpler supervisory screens.

The similar specifications of the hazard models estimated in each period suggest that this type of model is relatively stable over time. The finding that all of these hazard models produce accurate risk classifications out-of-sample is further evidence of model stability. Stability is a desirable property of any statistical early warning model because it means that frequent, costly re-specification is not required.

The hazard models are also found to be considerably more accurate than two simpler supervisory screens out-of-sample. In particular, the estimated models do a much better job of correctly flagging high-risk banks. Taken together the out-of-sample tests of classification accuracy suggest that this sort of statistical model is a promising, relatively low cost early warning tool.

References

Allison, P. *Survival Analysis Using the SAS System.* SAS Institute. Cary, NC (1995).

Board of Governors of the Federal Reserve System, Commercial Bank Examination Manual (May 1997).

Cleves, M. W. Gould, and R. Gutierrez. *An Introduction to Survival Analysis Using Stata.* STATA CORPORATION. College Station, Texas 2002.

Cole, R., B. Cornyn, and J. Gunther. "FIMS: A New Monitoring System for Banking Institutions." *Federal Reserve Bulletin* Board of Governors of the Federal Reserve System (January 1995).

Feldman, R. and J. Schmidt. "What Are CAMELS and Who Should Know?" *Fedgazette* Federal Reserve Bank of Minneapolis (January 1999).

Fissel, G. "Risk measurement, Actuarially-Fair Deposit insurance Premiums and the FDIC's Risk-Related Premium System." *FDIC Banking Review* 7 No. 1 (1994).

Gilbert, R., A. Meyer, and M. Vaughan. "The Role of Supervisory Screens and Econometric Models in Off-Site Surveillance." *Review* Federal Reserve Bank of St. Louis (November/December 1999).

Gropp, R., J. Vesala, and G. Vulpes. "Equity and Bond Market Signals as Leading Indicators of Bank Fragility." Working Paper No. 150 European Central Bank (June 2002).

Harvey, J. and J. Padget. "Subchapter S – A New Tool for Enhancing the Value of Community Banks." *Financial Industry Perspectives* Federal Reserve Bank of Kansas City (2000).

Hosmer, D. and S. Lemeshow. *Applied Survival Analysis.* John Wiley and Sons, Inc. New York (1999).

Lane, W., S. Looney, and J. Wansley. "An Application of the Cox Proportional Hazards Model to Bank Failure." *Journal of Banking and Finance* 10 (December 1986).

Office of the Comptroller of the Currency. Community Bank Supervision Comptroller's Handbook (July 2003).

Whalen, G. "A Proportional Hazards Model of Bank Failure: An Examination of its Usefulness as an Early Warning Tool." *Economic Review* 27 No. 1 Federal Reserve Bank of Cleveland (1991).

Wheelock, D. and P. Wilson. "Why Do Banks Disappear? The Determinants of U.S. Bank Failures and Acquisitions." *Review of Economics and Statistics* 82 No. 1 (February 2000).

Table 1

Hazard Models of the Probability of a CAMEL Downgrade

Variables	1997 Model		1998 Model		1999 Model	
	Coefficient	Z Stat	Coefficient	Z Stat	Coefficient	Z Stat
Total Equity/Total Assets	-0.183996	-4.73***	-0.206439	-4.02***	-0.131210	-2.53**
Total Nonperforming Loans/Total Loans	0.214103	6.87***	0.160075	4.38***		
Total Noncurrent Loans/Total Loans					0.406983	4.84***
Loans Past Due 30-89 Days/Total Loans					0.202640	3.34***
Loan Loss Provision/Total Assets	0.398585	3.41***	0.483349	3.04***	0.521865	4.91***
Commercial Loans/Total Assets	0.047535	4.91***	0.039966	3.36***	0.046174	4.63***
Loan Loss Reserves/Total Loans					-0.446415	-2.20**
Nonmaturity Deposits/Total Assets	-0.017326	-1.96**	-0.028127	-2.79***	-0.016395	-1.98**
Brokered Deposits/Total Assets	0.113064	5.19***	0.102267	4.22***	0.050417	1.80*
Other Borrowed Funds Mat. LT 1 Yr/Total Assets	0.046632	2.50**				
Total Investment Securities/Total Assets					-0.035877	-3.23***
Pledged Securities/Total Investment Securities			0.012869	3.02***		
Pretax Net Income/Total Assets	-0.194596	-4.13***	-0.762178	-4.93***	-0.270941	-2.66***
Log of Total Assets	-0.4117099	-3.37***	-0.2864452	-2.03**	-0.3791828	-2.95***
Net Gains on Loan Sales/Total Assets	0.829428	5.18***	0.6281741	1.70*		
Assets Repricing in 15 Years or More/Total Assets			,0214943	1.67*		
Dummy Variable=1 if M Rating > CAMELS	0.8508825	3.43***	1.59573	5.76***	0.6994819	1.78*
LL	-719.37		-552.17		-505.14	
LR chi2	176.40***		155.00***		146.41***	
8 Qtr Baseline Survival Probability	0.9722		0.9834		0.9794	
Number of Banks in Estimation Sample	2082		1923		1823	
Number of Downgrades During Estimation Period	107		84		78	

Table 2

Type I and Type II Error Rates
With Watch Lists of Varying Sizes
1997 Model
2001 Year-end Data, DGDs 2002:Q2 - 2004:Q1
1637 Banks: 81 DGD/1556 NDGD

Watch List Size	Type I Error Rate	Type II Error Rate
300	.383(31/81)	.161(250/1556)
350	.346(28/81)	.191(297/1556)
400	.321(26/81)	.222(345/1556)
450	.296(24/81)	.253(393/1556)
500	.284(23/81)	.284(442/1556)

Table 3

Type I and Type II Error Rates
With Watch Lists of Varying Sizes
1998 Model
2001 Year-end Data, DGDs 2002:Q2 - 2004:Q1
1637 Banks: 81 DGD/1556 NDGD

Watch List Size	Type I Error Rate	Type II Error Rate
300	.407(33/81)	.162(252/1556)
350	.395(32/81)	.193(301/1556)
400	.370(30/81)	.224(349/1556)
450	.333(27/81)	.254(396/1556)
500	.309(25/81)	.285(444/1556)

Table 4

Type I and Type II Error Rates
With Watch Lists of Varying Sizes
1999 Model
2001 Year-end Data, DGDs 2002:Q2 - 2004:Q1
1637 Banks: 81 DGD/1556 NDGD

Watch List Size	Type I Error Rate	Type II Error Rate
300	.395(32/81)	.161(251/1556)
350	.358(29/81)	.192(298/1556)
400	.296(24/81)	.220(343/1556)
450	.272(22/81)	.251(391/1556)
500	.272(22/81)	.283(441/1556)

Table 5

Type I and Type II Error Rates
With Watch Lists of Varying Sizes
1997 Model, 1999 Weights
2001 Year-end Data, DGDs 2002:Q2 - 2004:Q1
1637 Banks: 81 DGD/1556 NDGD

Watch List Size	Type I Error Rate	Type II Error Rate
300	.407(33/81)	.162(252/1556)
350	.370(30/81)	.192(299/1556)
400	.296(24/81)	.220(343/1556)
450	.296(24/81)	.253(393/1556)
500	.284(23/81)	.284(442/1556)

Table 6

Type I and Type II Error Rates
With Watch Lists of Varying Sizes
Canary Static Sum + SCOR
2001 Year-end Data, DGDs 2002:Q2 - 2004:Q1
1637 Banks: 81 DGD/1556 NDGD

Watch List Size	Type I Error Rate	Type II Error Rate
300	.667(54/81)	.175(273/1556)
350	.593(48/81)	.204(317/1556)
400	.531(43/81)	.233(362/1556)
450	.494(40/81)	.263(409/1556)
500	.420(34/81)	.291(453/1556)

Table 7

Type I and Type II Error Rates
With Watch Lists of Varying Sizes
Canary Static/Change Sum + SCOR
2001 Year-end Data, DGDs 2002:Q2 - 2004:Q1
1637 Banks: 81 DGD/1556 NDGD

Watch List Size	Type I Error Rate	Type II Error Rate
300	.716(58/81)	.177(277/1556)
350	.605(49/81)	.204(318/1556)
400	.494(40/81)	.230(359/1556)
450	.444(36/81)	.259(405/1556)
500	.432(35/81)	.291(454/1556)

www.ingramcontent.com/pod-product-compliance
Lightning Source LLC
Chambersburg PA
CBHW052025280526
45793CB00005B/1130

9781505308914